11.95

INTERIM SITE

SO-DXN-483

3 1192 00723 3727

x959.9 Stewa.G

Stewart, Gail, 1949-

The Philippines /

c1991.

THE PHILIPPINES

by
Gail B. Stewart

CRESTWOOD HOUSE
New York

Maxwell Macmillan Canada
Toronto

Maxwell Macmillan International
New York Oxford Singapore Sydney

Library of Congress Cataloging-in-Publication Data

Stewart, Gail, date.

The Philippines / by Gail Stewart. — 1st ed.

p. cm. — (Places in the news)

Includes index.

Summary: Examines the political scene in the Philippines during the years of the Marcos dictatorship and considers the problems and prospects of the administration of Corazon Aquino.

ISBN 0-89686-659-9

1. Philippines—Politics and government—1946– —Juvenile literature. [1. Philippines—Politics and government—1946–] I. Title. II. Series: Stewart, Gail, date. Places in the news.

DS686 .5.S82   1991

959.904—dc20

91-11143
CIP
AC

Photo Credits

Photos courtesy of AP—World Wide Photos

Copyright © 1991 Crestwood House, Macmillan Publishing Company

All rights reserved. No part of this book may be reproduced or transmitted in any form or by any means, electronic or mechanical, including photocopying, recording, or by any information storage and retrieval system, without permission in writing from the Publisher.

CRESTWOOD HOUSE

Macmillan Publishing Company
866 Third Avenue
New York, NY 10022

Maxwell Macmillan Canada, Inc.
1200 Eglinton Avenue East
Suite 200
Don Mills, Ontario M3C 3N1

Macmillan Publishing Company is part of the Maxwell Communication Group of Companies.

Produced by Flying Fish Studio

Printed in the United States of America

First edition

10 9 8 7 6 5 4 3 2 1

CONTENTS

THE PHILIPPINES IN THE NEWS

In February 1986 the Republic of the Philippines was making headlines all around the world. The president of the country, Ferdinand Marcos, was forced to flee to the United States.

During his years in office Marcos had used his power to change many of the laws in the Philippines. He became a dictator—more powerful than anyone else in his country. He used the army to enforce his will. He stole fortunes from the treasury of the Philippines. Even when there were elections, Marcos ordered his advisers to see that no one else would win. The results were always the same—a landslide victory for Marcos.

But in 1986 all of that changed. An election was held, one that Marcos was confident of winning. His opponent was a woman named Corazon Aquino. Although her husband had once been involved in politics, she had never held office. She was, as one official put it, "a complete and total rookie."

Corazon Aquino waves to her cheering audience after winning the 1986 presidential election in the Philippines.

Admitting Defeat

Aquino did not have the same kind of power Marcos had. But she appealed to the Filipino people. She hated Marcos and the bullying tactics he used on the people. In her campaign Aquino used the slogan "People Power." She wanted Filipinos to remember that they did have a say in their government, no matter what Marcos thought.

Although Aquino won a clear majority of the votes, Marcos declared himself the winner of the election. But his support had dwindled. There were mass demonstrations against him in Manila, the nation's capital. And a large portion of the military had turned against him. Soldiers in his army were fighting among themselves. Several key advisers abandoned Marcos, calling for a new government.

U.S. President Ronald Reagan contacted Marcos, urging him to step aside. Reagan told Marcos that if he used his power as a dictator this time, it might result in a bloody civil war.

In the end Marcos accepted defeat. Although he never admitted that he had done anything wrong, he fled the Philippines. He and his wife, Imelda, hurriedly left for Hawaii aboard a U.S. Air Force jet.

Corazon Aquino was officially the new president of the Philippines. "People Power" had overpowered the dictator. All over the country, excited Filipinos dressed in bright yellow, Aquino's favorite color. Many waved yellow flags in her honor.

"We are free!" yelled one woman in Manila. "We are done with the dictator, and we can hold up our heads again!"

From the United States Reagan sent congratulations to the new president. "Today the Filipino people celebrate the triumph of democracy, and the world celebrates with them," he announced.

President Aquino visits with President Reagan shortly after her election. Reagan voiced great confidence in the new leader.

"It Won't Be Easy"

Aquino was popular, both in her country and in the United States. She visited America in the fall of 1986. One of her goals was to convince the United States to give more financial aid to the Philippines.

On the day she visited Washington, D.C., several members of Congress waved yellow handkerchiefs. Many wore yellow ties or yellow shirts. Two hundred yellow rosebuds were handed out to members of Congress.

Speaking before Congress, Corazon Aquino flashes her familiar victory sign.

Her speech was persuasive. She urged the United States to invest in the Philippines. She assured Americans that there were no more of Marcos's men running the government "with their hands in the till."

Even those U.S. officials who had been skeptical of Aquino seemed convinced she would be a good president. "I am terribly impressed," said one of Reagan's staff members. "I am also terribly surprised. She has the confident manner of one who has been running the ship for 20 years. She doesn't flinch, she doesn't avoid the hard questions. It won't be easy for her, but I'll bet she can do it."

And President Reagan gave her a vote of confidence. He told Aquino "that all America wants the Philippine democracy to succeed and prosper." And he promised, "We'll do what we can to help."

8

Four Years Later

In late 1990 the Philippines was still making headlines. But this time the reason was not the fall of a dictator. And it was not the Cinderella story of a political rookie beating a powerful ruler.

Instead newspapers were reporting attempts by some Filipinos to force President Aquino out of office. Since her election in 1986 there have been several attempts by rebels to overthrow her. Some of these attempted coups, or sudden takeovers of the government, were directed by her own trusted advisers!

President Aquino had promised the people that big changes would take place. She wanted to give more power to the poor of her country. She wanted to work out peaceful solutions with the various rebel groups in the Philippines. And, as she promised the U.S. Congress back in 1986, she wanted to begin a period of growth and rebuilding.

Worry in the Philippines

But something has gone wrong in the Philippines. There is a restless, worried mood among the people. They feel that Corazon Aquino has not lived up to the promises she made.

There is increasing terrorism and violence by the very groups Aquino wanted to work with. The communist rebels, for example, have driven all 261 Peace Corps workers out of the country. And since 1987 three members of the American military stationed in the Philippines have been murdered.

Many Filipinos are also angry that corruption and dirty deals are still part of their government. "I thought we had put an end to that when Cory [Corazon Aquino's nickname] became president," said one teacher from Manila. "But there are still thieves in her government, taking what belongs to us all. I don't believe Cory is dishonest. But she does not punish those of her advisers who are cheating us."

A news commentator in Manila agrees. "She is sincere, moral and honest. But the presidency is obviously beyond her capabilities, beyond her experience."

In the United States there is worry that Aquino is not the strong leader everyone thought she would be. One aide to President George Bush said, "We're committed to her, and we hope that she'll muddle through. But she simply doesn't know how to govern."

What Has Gone Wrong?

Whatever the reasons, people in the Philippines have lost confidence in their president. A recent news poll showed that less than half believe she is doing a good job.

Aquino has been quoted as saying that people expect too much too soon. She thinks that many of the country's problems will take years to solve. Marcos, she says, did so much damage that no one could repair it in only four years. She says that a great deal will be accomplished by the time her term is up in 1992.

But many in the Philippines and the United States wonder if President Aquino will last that long. With rebel soldiers planning coups, her future is, as one U.S. official says, "not exactly filled with hope and promise."

10

What has happened? How did things change from cheering crowds in yellow chanting "Cory, Cory"? What has gone wrong for President Aquino and the Philippines?

While some Filipinos are unhappy with Aquino's government, many still support her and hope that she can bring prosperity and stability to the nation.

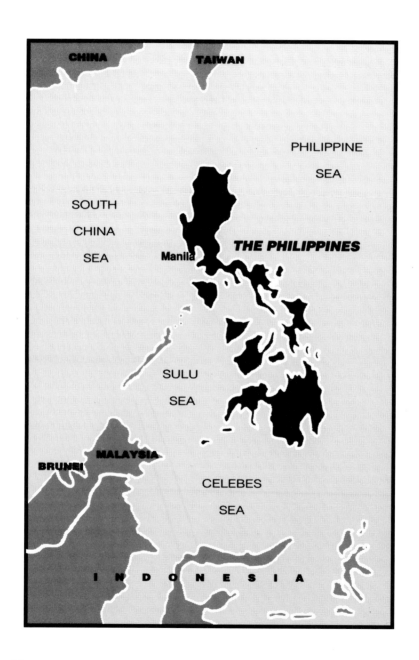

CHINA

TAIWAN

PHILIPPINE

SEA

SOUTH

CHINA

SEA

Manila

THE PHILIPPINES

SULU

SEA

BRUNEI

MALAYSIA

CELEBES

SEA

I N D O N E S I A

THE BEGINNINGS OF TROUBLE

It would be impossible to understand the troubles in the Philippines by looking only at the last four years. Many of the current difficulties can be traced back to President Marcos's time. Some go back even further—to the days when other countries controlled the Philippines.

A Nation of Islands

Many people don't know that the Republic of the Philippines is actually a large number of separate islands. In all there are more than 7,100! Most of these are tiny—less than one square mile in area—and no one lives on them.

There are about a thousand islands on which people do live. But only a small number are large enough to be important politically. The largest islands are Luzon, in the north, and Mindanao, in the south. These are the islands on which the majority of the nation's 60 million people live.

People who study politics know that geography has a big effect on how a country develops over the centuries. Because the Philippines is made up of thousands of islands, it did not develop one main culture. The islands kept the people apart. People on one island were not the same as people on other islands. Different religions, different customs and different languages grew up over the centuries. Even today more than 87 dialects, or local languages, are spoken by the Filipinos!

13

Spanish explorer Ferdinand Magellan first landed in the Philippines in 1521. Some years later, Spain conquered the islands.

Influences from Around the World

But the long-ago Filipinos were not cut off from the rest of the world. Historians know that around A.D. 700 traders from the Orient visited the Philippines. Chinese traders did business in the Philippines, as did Arabs. (In fact, the Arabs introduced the religion of Islam to some Filipinos.)

These visitors influenced the island people, but there were no wars. Neither Arab nor Chinese leaders gave much thought to conquering the islands.

But in 1521 everything changed. The Spanish explorer Ferdinand Magellan landed on the islands. Three more Spanish expeditions followed Magellan across the Pacific. The commander of the third, Ruy López de Villalobos, named the islands the "Felipinas" after Prince Philip of Spain. In 1565 the king of Spain sent another expedition to conquer and colonize the "Felipinas."

The Spanish established permanent settlements on the islands. On Luzon they made Manila a central port for their ships. From there they carried on trade with China and other nations in the Far East.

The conquerors brought their religion with them too. They were Roman Catholics, and they forced the mostly pagan Filipinos to convert. Only the Muslims—those who followed the religion of Islam taught by the Arabs—did not convert.

A Cruel System

One of the worst things the Spanish brought to the Philippines was a new economic system. This changed the way all Filipinos lived and worked.

Before the Spanish colonized the islands, most of the people were farmers. They lived in scattered villages where the land was shared by everyone. Each village was able to produce almost everything it needed.

But the Spanish wanted to make money from their colony.

They took the land away from the Filipinos and made them work for Spanish landlords. The Spanish also required the Filipinos to labor on public works of various kinds, especially cutting timber and building ships for them.

By the 18th century the Spanish landlords had completely reorganized agriculture in the islands. Now there were huge plantations where hundreds, or even thousands, of Filipinos did all the work to raise crops such as tobacco, sugar and abaca (a plant used in making rope). The Spanish exported these crops for a great deal of money. They allowed the Filipinos to work small plots of land on which they could grow just enough food to feed their families. But the Filipinos were not allowed to own any land.

The Filipinos had many other restrictions. They could not vote or hold office. They were not allowed to pursue higher education until the end of the 17th century. They had to pay taxes of various kinds to Spain.

A New Owner for the Philippines

It is not hard to understand why the Filipino people resented the Spanish colonists. The Filipinos did not want to be "owned" by another group of people. Rebellions and uprisings became frequent in the Philippines.

In 1898 the United States defeated Spain in the Spanish-American War. After the U.S. Navy destroyed the Spanish fleet anchored in Manila Bay, the American admiral George Dewey encouraged the Filipinos to continue the revolt against the Spanish that had begun two years earlier. The Filipinos believed that the United States only wanted to help them gain their freedom.

However, they were disappointed. As part of the peace settlement Spain gave up some of its possessions to the United States. The Philippines was one of the lands that changed hands. As of 1898, the Philippines had a new owner—the United States!

War, and Waiting

Many Filipinos were angry at being given away. Led by Emilio Aquinaldo, a former schoolteacher, they fought the American troops that came to the Philippines. The struggle was fierce. More than 200,000 Filipino civilians were killed. In 1901 Aquinaldo was captured, and the fighting finally ended in 1902. The United States had won.

The United States said that it planned to eventually grant the Philippines independence. However, U.S. leaders thought that the Filipino people were not ready to govern themselves yet. It was first necessary, they said, for the Filipinos to develop a democratic system of government. Not surprisingly, the Filipinos were instructed to model their new government after that of the United States.

American advisers helped Filipinos write a constitution. They assisted them in creating a two-house legislature, much like Congress. The public school system was expanded, and hundreds of Americans came to the Philippines to teach Filipinos English. The Philippines quickly took on a very American look—even down to the white columns on government buildings!

But the Americans did nothing to help the poor farmers of the Philippines. The system of a few large landowners controlling the majority of the people continued.

The city of Manila lies in ruins after the bombings of World War II.

Free at Last

World War II had a devastating effect on the Philippines. Despite heroic resistance by the Filipinos, the Japanese occupied the islands in 1942. By the time U.S. General Douglas MacArthur liberated the Philippines in 1944, the countryside had been plundered and Manila lay in ruins. But the date for Philippine independence had been set since 1934. And despite all the problems facing the new nation, no one wanted to postpone it.

So, on July 4, 1946, the United States granted independence to the islands. As of that date the nation was known as the Republic of the Philippines. The United States pledged that it would give aid to the new republic. At the same time, Filipino leaders would allow the United States to keep military bases there.

The future looked promising for the Philippines in 1946. For centuries Filipinos had looked forward to independence. They wanted to be able to work together to solve their own problems.

But troubles ahead would threaten the new republic. And this time the problems would come not from outsiders, but from people within the Philippines.

EARLY YEARS OF A NEW REPUBLIC

In 1946 the Philippines had its independence—but the country was in ruins. During the war years entire villages had been wiped out. Stores, churches and farm fields were rubble. The capital city, Manila, which also contained most of the country's factories, hospitals and universities, was almost totally destroyed.

Trouble Everywhere

Recovery from the war was slow and difficult. Food was in very short supply. Farmers had had no luck growing crops during the war, for their fields were battlegrounds. The tiny amount of food that was available was not nearly enough for the population. It was impossible to ship food from one place to another, for roads had been bombed.

Sickness raged among the people. The lack of good nutrition meant that many Filipinos were not strong enough to fight off illness. Diseases such as malaria struck whole villages. Only the hardiest people survived.

Even in the biggest towns and cities, public services did not exist. No buses, no garbage collection, no water or power plants made life easier for the Filipinos. Until the nation could get the most basic necessities, these things would simply have to wait.

Poverty was everywhere. Many who had no food stole it from others. Packs of criminals roamed the islands, preying on families lucky enough to have something of value.

The Rise of the Huks

After World War II there was a rise in communist activity in the Philippines. Communism is an economic and political system under which all businesses and property are owned by the state. There is no private property. Communists believe that in this way all people are equal. No one has more than anyone else. There are no poor people and no millionaires under a true communist system.

The communists in the Philippines were angry because of the unjust system of land ownership. They believed that a new system of government, the communist one, would eliminate poverty. No longer would a few rich landowners control all the money and power in the Philippines. There would be an equal distribution of land, money and power among the millions of poor peasants.

The communists of the Philippines were known as the People's Liberation Army, or Huks. (This is an abbreviation in Tagalog, a language of the Philippines.) The Huks formed guerrilla groups. They terrorized the wealthy of the Philippines and attacked government soldiers who tried to stop them. As with any guerrilla group, the Huks wore no uniforms and did not fight in regiments.

They attacked in small groups of two or three. Because of these tactics, it was very hard for the government of the Philippines to control them.

A Difficult Job

With all these problems facing the new republic, elected officials had a very difficult job. One of the best leaders was president from 1953 to 1957. His name was Ramón Magsaysay.

Magsaysay was able to stop a lot of the guerrilla activity among the Huks. He offered them a deal if they would put down their weapons. He granted them pardons, or promises that they would not be punished for their crimes. Magsaysay also gave them some land. In return the Huks promised they would cease their attacks on the government and other Filipinos.

Magsaysay died in a plane crash in 1957. Many historians think that if he had lived he would have accomplished a great deal more. He had the respect of most Filipinos—supporters and enemies alike. He understood the plight of the poor. He knew that military action alone would not stop the activities of groups like the Huks. Social reforms—changes in the way people live—had to take place too.

Marcos Becomes President

Not every leader had the abilities of Magsaysay. Those who succeeded him were not as strong or as capable of commanding respect. Some government officials were corrupt, taking money or favors in return for granting privileges to the wealthy. Others simply were overwhelmed by the difficulties of solving the problems in the Philippines.

In 1965 a 47-year-old lawyer named Ferdinand Marcos became president. Marcos was determined to be a strong president. He was fairly popular with Filipinos. He supported reforms that would help farmers be more productive. He worked hard to start public-works projects, especially the building of bridges and roads.

Marcos did accomplish some things during his first four-year term. However, there were many who did not think he had done enough to help the poor. When Marcos ran for reelection in 1969, many people supported his opponent. Marcos won, but the election was far from orderly and civilized. There was a great deal of violence. Bloody battles erupted between government soldiers and Filipinos who called for an end to Marcos's rule. In all, 109 people were killed.

Troubles on the Rise

Marcos's second term in office was far more difficult than his first. "The election of 1969 was an omen of things to come," says one Filipino. "The street fighting and killing was an indication that troubles for Marcos were on the rise."

Poverty, for instance, was at an all-time high. Historians estimate that in 1965 about 400 families controlled everything in the Philippines. They owned the land and employed millions of poor Filipinos to help them farm it. With their wealth these families could afford to buy anything. Many bribed soldiers, members of Congress and anyone else whose help they needed.

Ferdinand Marcos addresses a crowd. At first, the notorious leader was popular with the Filipinos.

Poverty caused other problems too. One was overcrowding. Many who could not make a living in the country moved to the cities seeking jobs. But when they got there, they often found conditions equally as bad. They were forced to live in the streets, or under bridges, or in cardboard shacks on the outskirts of town. Because of the crowded conditions, disease spread quickly. Being poor in the cities of the Philippines meant being unemployed and sick.

"Marcos did nothing to help the poor," says a nurse who works in Manila. "He could not afford it. If he worked to improve their lives, he risked offending the rich Filipinos. How could he do that? It was all right to talk about helping the poor, but talk was all. There were too many people whom Marcos did not want to anger."

"Out, Out, U.S.A.!"

Another problem Marcos faced had to do with the Americans. When the United States acquired the Philippines, it established military bases there. The Philippines is very close to the mainland of Asia, and keeping troops there was important to U.S. defense strategy.

When the Philippines became independent in 1946, the United States insisted that the two main bases remain. Clark Air Base and Subic Bay Military Base were too important to the United States to shut down. In return for allowing the bases to remain, the United States paid the government of the Philippines $550 million each year.

The money was important to the Philippines. But many Filipinos resented Americans being there. To them the military bases were a constant reminder that their nation was under the thumb of the United States.

During Marcos's second term in office there were many demonstrations against the United States. Filipinos chanting "Out, out, U.S.A.!" and holding large anti-American signs marched outside Marcos's palace in Manila.

"If we are independent, then why are American soldiers patrolling the skies and waters of the Philippines?" asked one protester. "We asked questions like this, but we got no answers

Demonstrators protest the presence of American military bases in the Philippines.

from Marcos. He was loyal to the United States. We thought he was more patriotic to America than to the Philippines. Perhaps the money made him a patriot."

Rewriting the Rules

Marcos's second term should have been his last. That was the rule in the constitution of the Philippines. Like an American president, the president of the Philippines was allowed only two consecutive terms in office.

But Ferdinand Marcos was anxious to remain in power. He did not want to give up the presidency in 1973. The only way he could remain president was to change the rules. And that is just what he did.

In 1972 Marcos declared martial law. That means that there was an emergency—a crisis that made it necessary to stop normal government. According to Marcos, there were many reasons to impose martial law. The rising number of demonstrators against the U.S. military bases was one reason. Another was the increase in guerrilla activity by the Huks and other anti-government groups.

Martial law is a big change in the way a government works. Marcos scrapped the constitution and ordered a new one written. With his new "emergency" powers, Marcos, his wife, Imelda, and a few trusted friends controlled the nation.

Many Filipinos didn't believe Marcos's reasons for imposing martial law. "It was a power move, pure and simple," says a history professor from the Philippines. "He was in danger of losing his support, and he wanted to keep being president— forever. The story he gave the Filipino people—that he needed to 'protect' us from enemies in our country—that was all rubbish."

Silencing the People

Marcos wanted to make sure that there was no chance of a move against him. As part of martial law he made many democratic rights illegal. For instance, Filipino people were not allowed to meet together for political reasons. Town or village meetings were against the law.

The radio and newspapers were seized by the government. Nothing could be printed or reported that did not meet the approval of Marcos.

Another part of martial law was Marcos's enemy list. He ordered the army to arrest anyone who was suspected of making threats against him or of stirring up trouble. The list included communist and Muslim rebels.

However, there were plenty of other people on the list. Some were guilty of nothing more than criticizing Marcos or of disagreeing with his policies. Political rivals too were jailed. Thousands of these "enemies" were beaten or tortured. The situation in the Philippines was frightening and violent. And there seemed to be nothing anyone could do about it.

Ninoy Aquino

One man who dared speak out against Marcos was Benigno Aquino. He was called Ninoy by his friends. Aquino was a rising star in Philippine politics in the Marcos years. He was young, energetic and sympathetic to the poor. Many believed that Aquino would be a good president when Marcos's term ended in 1973.

But when martial law began Aquino criticized Marcos. Marcos

Benigno Aquino, Marcos's biggest threat, was a rising political star before he was imprisoned for seven years.

put him on the enemy list, and Aquino was jailed. He remained in jail for seven and a half years.

"Ninoy was Marcos's biggest threat," states one reporter from the Philippines. "Everyone believed he would be the next president. Ninoy loved people, loved to work hard. It would have been impossible for anyone to beat him in an honest fight. So Marcos had to abandon honesty and fairness. Jail was the only way Ninoy could be silenced."

In 1980 Ninoy suffered a serious heart attack in prison. Doctors said that the only way to save his life was to perform triple-bypass surgery, a complicated procedure. Doctors in the United States performed this surgery often, and Ninoy's doctors recommended flying him to America.

So in 1980 Ninoy, his wife, Corazon, and their children moved to the United States. Ninoy's surgery was successful. The family settled comfortably into their new country.

The End of Martial Law

By 1981 Marcos found that his actions were being criticized by more and more people. U.S. officials were embarrassed by his undemocratic tactics. After all, the Philippine government was supposedly modeled on that of the United States. Locking up enemies and jailing critics was hardly democratic!

The Catholic Church was also critical. Many priests called on Marcos to stop persecuting innocent people. They demanded an end to what they saw as human-rights crimes.

In 1981 Marcos bowed to the pressure. He lifted martial law. He assured the people of the Philippines that the danger had passed. The government was safe, and he would extend more liberties to the media and citizens of the Philippines. However, critics protested that Marcos had not changed very much.

"He was still a dictator," states a woman from the island of Mindanao. "He relaxed the martial law, but his army didn't relax. They still threatened us. Anyone who wanted to help the country by changing things was beaten up or worse. Nothing much had changed, and we all knew it."

In 1983 Ninoy Aquino also had had enough. Although he was safe in the United States, he wanted to return to the Philippines. He knew he was in great danger. His family asked him not to go, but they realized he felt an obligation. Aquino wanted to help his people. By running for office against Marcos, he might be able to do just that.

Murder

Aquino flew to Manila under a false name. He did not want any of Marcos's men to have advance warning that he was coming. However, word leaked to the Philippine government that Aquino was returning. As he was getting off the plane, Aquino was shot in the back of the head and killed.

The people of the Philippines were outraged. The government acted outraged too. Marcos told the people that a communist gunman had committed the murder. He called for a full investigation into the killing of Ninoy Aquino.

Returning to the Philippines to run against Marcos, Benigno Aquino (in white) was assassinated as he got off the plane.

But the investigating committee found out otherwise. After a year of gathering facts, the committee announced that Aquino had in fact been murdered by government soldiers. The armed forces' chief of staff and 24 other soldiers were accused of taking part in a carefully planned plot to kill Aquino. Because the military men worked so closely with Marcos, the president also looked guilty to many Filipinos.

In 1985 the men went to trial before a special court made up entirely of people loyal to Marcos. All of the soldiers were found not guilty.

Filipinos were angrier than ever. They had thought that Aquino's murderers would be brought to trial, and they were. Yet the murderers would not be punished. It was not fair—not to Ninoy, and not to the people of the Philippines who wanted justice.

Marcos knew that people were suspicious. He wanted to restore confidence in his government. He announced that there would be an election in 1986. Filipinos could vote for the candidate of their choice.

"Marcos thought he would be seen as an open, interested man," says one historian. "By calling for an election, he was trying to show that he had nothing to fear. However, it was a decision that would blow up in his face."

THE CHALLENGES OF CORY AQUINO

Marcos thought that the election would be easy to win. Although there were many people who did not support him, he had two things working in his favor.

First, there were many people who wanted to run against him. With so many opponents it would be difficult for any one of them to get enough support to beat him. And second, Marcos knew that he had a corrupt government. His soldiers and his assistants could rig the election so that he would win.

Marcos's Opponent

With just a few weeks until the election, the race narrowed. All of the opposition parties were able to agree on one candidate to challenge Marcos—Corazon Aquino. She was anxious to carry on her husband's work, and some of her own.

At first Cory Aquino did not believe that she could win. However, as the election drew closer more and more Filipinos pledged their support. More than a million voters said that if she put her name on the ballot, they would vote for her.

Aquino got serious about the campaign. She sent the word to Marcos in her speeches and her campaign literature—she would not be threatened. "This is the voice of the people," she said in a speech. "Mr. Marcos, we will not be intimidated by you. You cannot murder each and every one of us—there are too many."

Corazon Aquino successfully defeated Marcos in 1986 and continued the fight begun by her husband to bring democracy to the nation.

"Vote Early, Vote Often"

There was a saying in the Philippines about elections—"Vote early, vote often." The saying was meant to be funny, making a joke of the corruption in the elections. However, the saying was almost true.

People were often paid to vote a certain way. If they did not comply, they were beaten. Soldiers made no secret of threatening voters. The candidate who won the election was not necessarily the one who received the most votes. Often, it was the one who controlled the army.

Because all these things were known, there was concern on the part of many people that the election would not be fair. The United States agreed to send impartial observers. Their job was to watch the election and to make sure that there were no threats or bribes.

When the votes were counted, Cory Aquino had won. However, the National Assembly (controlled by Marcos) declared Marcos the winner. The U.S. observers protested that there had been some tampering with the results. They also declared Aquino the winner.

In two different parts of Manila, two separate swearing-in ceremonies took place. Aquino's supporters cheered as she took the oath of office. And Marcos held a hasty ceremony with a small group of followers on hand.

There couldn't be two presidents. What would happen next?

While Aquino's victory pleased the majority of Filipinos, some wanted the return of Ferdinand Marcos.

The Truth Comes Out

President Reagan and other world leaders urged Marcos to step down. At first he refused, saying that he was the rightful president. However, Aquino's supporters staged continual mass demonstrations in Manila. And when a large portion of the military turned against him, Marcos finally changed his mind. He and his family fled to Hawaii.

Ferdinand Marcos lands in Hawaii after fleeing the Philippines.

Some of the thousands of dresses found in Imelda Marcos's storerooms

Marcos took with him crates and suitcases filled with money. It had been suspected for a long time that he and his wife had been cheating the people—stealing money that belonged to the government. Now, it seemed, those suspicions had been proved true. Customs officials estimated that about $5 million in cash was crammed in Marcos's luggage!

This stash was just the tip of the iceberg, according to officials. It was estimated that Marcos's wealth topped $3 billion. Much of the money was in overseas bank accounts and investments.

After the Marcoses left the Philippines, Filipinos got a glimpse of what the couple's life had been like. Film crews went to the palace from which the president and his wife had hurriedly fled. The man whose official presidential salary was only $5,200 a year had lived a very rich life indeed. In one shot the crews showed Imelda Marcos's shoe closet. In it were 1,700 pairs of expensive shoes!

Corazon Aquino reviews the troops.

A Good Start

The new president, Cory Aquino, knew she had a lot of work to do. Because of Marcos, the nation was in financial trouble. The Filipino people were bitter about the way they had been cheated.

Aquino got off to a fairly good start as president. She vowed that she would try to get the courts to force Marcos to return the money he had taken. She also began a program to strengthen the economy. New housing had to be built and public services like road maintenance had to be improved.

She also restored many of the freedoms that had been lost under Marcos's rule. She made sure the Congress and courts were functioning again. She gave freedom of speech back to the media. She also encouraged Filipinos to meet in political assemblies, to decide what they needed in their communities.

In the first months of her presidency it seemed that Aquino would be a strong leader. The United States and other nations had been worried toward the end of Marcos's rule. They had not felt comfortable investing in or loaning money to the Philippines, for the nation did not seem stable. But under President Aquino there was a feeling of optimism and security. Because of this, loans and financial aid were given to the new government. For the first time in many years the Philippines seemed to be on track.

Too Good to Be True

But the good feelings of "People Power" did not last. It became clear in the late 1980s that Aquino's government suffered from many of the same problems as Marcos's.

Poverty is, according to many Filipinos, the number one problem in their country. Two-thirds of Filipinos live in rural areas. They do their best to scratch out a living, but almost all are poor. They live in shacks without telephones, electricity or running water. They go to bed hungry every night.

Poverty is the greatest problem facing Aquino's government as it tries to rebuild the Philippine economy.

Marcos was unable—or unwilling—to tackle the problem. But during her campaign Aquino said that helping the poor was one of her top priorities. She had devised a program that Filipinos were excited about. The program would allow Filipino farmers to buy land from the rich landowners. In this way they would become more independent and better able to support themselves.

But Aquino's program couldn't become law unless it passed in the Congress. Since the days of Marcos the Congress has been controlled by millionaires. None of them wanted the poor to take over land. So the program did not pass—at least not in the way Aquino had hoped.

"Congress changed the program. They took the teeth out of it," complains one woman who works with the poor in rural areas. "They managed to put loopholes and hidden escape clauses in the bill.

"Now instead of having to sell land, the landowners can sell shares in their plantations. Some of the shares can't even be cashed in for 30 years! Tell me, what good is that to the poor farmer who needs a plot of land?"

Hacienda Luisita

Aquino's critics say that she herself has not been fair to the poor. Aquino comes from a wealthy family that owns a 15,000-acre sugar plantation in the Philippines.

Hacienda Luisita, as it is called, is a perfect example of what Aquino says she wants to eliminate. The workers live in hot, stuffy, cramped shacks with their families. Pay is very low.

In contrast, the racehorses at Hacienda Luisita have fine quarters! Each horse has an airy, light space, far larger than any of the workers' shacks.

Some of the children who live on Hacienda Luisita, the Corazon family plantation

Aquino's family has taken advantage of the loophole in the law. They have refused to sell land to their workers—only paper shares. Those who supported Aquino and her "People Power" are angry.

"Is she different from Marcos?" asks one farm worker. "Maybe in some ways. I guess she tries to be honest, but it looks bad. She promised changes, she promised she'd help us. But millionaires are getting away with murder—and her own family is part of it! Why doesn't she start with them?"

Corruption

Another problem Aquino has not been able to solve is corruption. Bribes and theft by the military and government are costing the Philippines $2.5 billion each year. No one has accused Aquino herself of being corrupt. In fact, even her biggest critics admit she is honest. But she has done little to keep her government in line.

For instance, money is allotted by the Congress for roads and bridges. Sometimes a contractor will pay an inspector to say that the work has been done. However, the bridge may be only half done, or the road not built at all. The millions of dollars set aside for the project are divided among the dishonest contractors and inspectors.

Increasing Violence

Another worry in the Philippines is the unsteady government. Already there have been attempts to force Aquino out of office. Soldiers and government officials do not even hide the fact that they are part of the plots!

One reporter asked a general who had participated in an attempted coup if he planned on trying again. The general laughed. "Promising that I would never again take part in a coup would be like promising my wife I would never again drink beer. I cannot make promises like that!"

Such uncertainty has led to nervousness among investors. Companies that were eager to build factories or set up headquarters in the Philippines in 1986 are now worried. Of the 388 multinational corporations that were in Manila in 1985, only 120 are left. Many of these 120 are considering moving too.

Riot police attack student demonstrators in Manila. As the problems of the Philippines continue, violence and unrest increase.

What's Next?

No one is sure what will happen to Aquino's government. For now the people are confused. Many feel they have been misled by promises.

"She could not deliver what she promised," complains one father of five. "She tells us not to expect miracles. But it is only a miracle that will save our country now, I think."

Leaders of the United States and other nations say that they hope Aquino can get control of her government. But to do that she will need to be firm with her advisers and the military.

The Philippines has many problems that Cory Aquino did not create. However, the people who supported her in 1986 are expecting her to come up with some solutions.

"The answers are difficult," says a priest from Manila. "There are so many troubled people, so many hungry children. But at the same time, there are so many corrupt officials, so many greedy citizens. I feel very sorry for any honest leader who tries to make sense of it all."

In the days ahead the world will be watching Cory Aquino and her government. Will she be able to help her country solve its problems? Or will her term be ended before she gets a chance?

The future of the Philippines depends on the nation's ability to bridge the gap between the rich and the poor.

FACTS ABOUT THE PHILIPPINES

Capital: Manila

Population: 60 million

Form of government: Republic

Official languages: Filipino and English

Monetary unit: peso

Chief products:
    Agriculture: rice, corn, sugarcane, coconuts, tobacco
    Mineral ores: copper, gold, iron, chromite, nickel, coal

Glossary

communism *The political and economic system under which all property is owned by the state.*

coup *A sudden takeover of a government by an opposing group.*

guerrillas *Loosely knit groups of soldiers who use secrecy and sabotage to fight their enemies. The Huks were one guerrilla group in the Philippines.*

Huks *A group of communist rebels in the Philippines.*

Islam *The religion of Muslims, who believe in one God, Allah, and in the prophet Muhammad.*

martial law *An emergency measure with which a leader can halt normal freedoms among citizens.*

Muslim *One who follows the religion of Islam.*

pardon *A promise to forgive.*

Index